My Lord & My God

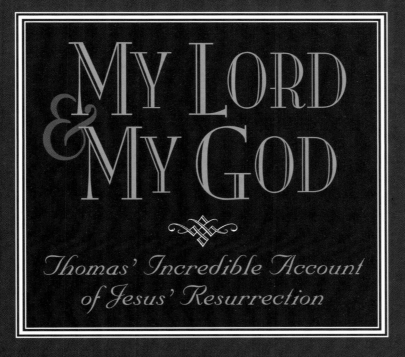

My Lord & My God

Thomas' Incredible Account
of Jesus' Resurrection

CALVIN MILLER
Illustrated by Ron DiCianni

Chariot VICTOR
PUBLISHING
A DIVISION OF COOK COMMUNICATIONS

To Deron Spoo,
whose resurrection confidence makes all the world around him
an unending and joyous Easter.
C.M.

To Randy Maid and Tim Botts,

who were instrumentally used of God to encourage me during the time

these illustrations were painted. It seems like yesterday. . . .

R.D.

—————————— ⚬⚭⚬ ——————————

This story is based on the account
of Jesus' resurrection found in the Gospels
Matthew, Mark, Luke, and John.

Chariot Books is an imprint of ChariotVictor Publishing,
a division of Cook Communications, Colorado Springs, Colorado 80918
Cook Communications, Paris, Ontario
Kingsway Communications, Eastbourne, England

MY LORD AND MY GOD
© 1998 by Calvin Miller for text and David C. Cook Publishing Company for illustrations.

Cover and interior design by Andrea Boven
Illustrations by Ron DiCianni
Editor: Jeannie Harmon

The art was originally created in 1989 by Ron DiCianni for Bible-in-Life Sunday School curriculum.

Scripture verses used on pages 5 and 32 are taken from the *Holy Bible: New International Version®.*
Copyright 1973, 1978, 1984 by International Bible Society.
Used by permission of Zondervan Publishing House. All rights reserved.

First printing, 1998
Printed in Singapore
02 01 00 99 98   5 4 3 2 1

Published in association with the literary agency of Alive Communications, Inc.,
1465 Kelly Johnson Blvd., Suite 320, Colorado Springs, CO 80920

Jesus answered,
"I am the way
and the truth
and the life."

John 14:6

Introduction

My story begins on a Thursday night just before Passover. The twelve of us met with Jesus in the upper room to observe the Jewish holiday dinner. The fare was traditional—a fine lamb with all the trimmings. The meal was so wonderful that I nearly forgot the fears I had felt earlier about going with Jesus to Jerusalem. I was the only one who objected to the trip and was outspoken on the matter. Jesus had many enemies there. I warned Him about going to Jerusalem at all. But I knew He would go, and I knew I would stand with Him whatever happened. Because the lamb that Thursday was so tasty and the fellowship so warm, I soon began to feel I had been nervous for no reason.

Then Jesus spoke. Suddenly, maybe even abruptly, He grew serious, "One of you is going to betray Me."

The statement settled like a slate sky over sunny Galilee. Our warm togetherness shattered! What did Jesus mean? Certainly none of us would betray the King of love Himself. The notion was so unthinkable, each found himself asking in disbelief, "Lord, surely not I?"

It was strange that none of us noticed Judas' silence, and even more unusual that we saw no immediate connection between Jesus' statement and Judas' hasty departure. He was the treasurer of our group and often went out to buy this or that to furnish our journey with what we needed. But it was late and the market was closed. We should have seen all that. We should have stopped Judas from leaving, but we did not.

The events of the next ten days tumbled over one another. Immediately we left the upper room and camped out that night in the garden of Gethsemane. We had camped there many times before but this night was different. There was something almost foreboding about the place. Moonlight filtered through the gnarled limbs of the olive trees leaving crooked shadows on the ground. Soon Judas arrived at Gethsemane with a detachment of guards. The military regalia made odd clanking noises as they entered the garden. Torches reflected off their brazen armor.

Suddenly I knew. We all knew. Judas was the traitor. I shuddered, feeling a tightening in the pit of my stomach. I knew that Judas' treachery was about to undo the world we loved.

Judas kissed Jesus!

A kiss mind you!

The kiss was a sign—the signal Judas offered to the guards to identify Jesus. I wish I could tell you what happened next. I cannot.

With that kiss of betrayal I fled into the night. My world fell apart. Escaping was easy. They weren't really after me. They were after Jesus. The dark shrubbery of the park was so dense I had only to slip through the surrounding thickets, and I was gone.

But with my getaway, came feelings of betrayal. I had, like all the rest, promised Jesus I would never leave Him. But when the chips were down we ran—all of us.

How I hated myself.

In but a few hours, Jesus was hanging by His hands. It took Him many hours after that to die. And die He did. I won't describe the ordeal of death by crucifixion for the cruelty of such executions is sheer horror. But I will say it was a relief when He finally died. He was taken from the cross and placed in the tomb of Joseph of Arimathea.

The light of the world went out that Friday afternoon. All I had ever found valuable in life was worthless. Jesus was dead, and His dying had left a deadness in the center of my soul.

Chapter One

Jesus was buried in such haste that His body was not properly prepared. Thus it was that Mary Magdalene and another woman went to the tomb right after sunrise on the first day of the week. They were taking burial spices to complete the process of embalming. As they hurried through the early morning mist of Sunday, they were preoccupied by a single thought. Who will roll away the stone?

But when they got there, to their surprise, the stone had been rolled away. The body of Jesus was gone! They were struck by a horrible possibility—could there have been a grave robbery? Their desire to put spices in His burial garment died with the realization that His body had been stolen.

All these things I know only by hearsay for I was not there, . . . sadly, I was not there.

Chapter Two

Mary Magdalene is the most emotional woman I have ever known. Her behavior, after finding the empty tomb, went beyond hysteria. She ran to the apostles crying breathlessly, "The tomb is empty, the tomb is empty. There's been a grave robbery!"

Mary had absolutely no proof of this. She just started the story. I had not seen her so upset since the day Jesus cast the demons out of her. After this miracle, she was clearly a different person, peaceful, appearing as one in love with the very Source of all love.

She was rich too, often slipping money to Judas to help support Jesus' ministry. She was one of the few I knew who could afford burial spices. But when the body of Jesus came up missing, she seemed to take on a new desperation. She couldn't deal with the fact that the body of her Lord was gone.

Her frantic report got the disciples very worked up.

"Who's gonna check this out?" asked one of the disciples.

Before there could be an answer, Peter jumped up and ran out the door. John bar Zebedee did too.

"Where are you going?" cried one of the apostles.

Neither Peter nor John answered. They just ran.

Mary's hysteria spawned a kind of madness. From that point on, mass lunacy seemed the appropriate way to behave.

Jesus' tomb was empty, and while Peter and John had no idea why they were running it seemed better to run than not to run. Sometimes in life you gotta run, I guess. When the world is upside down, walking is too slow. ❧

Chapter Three

While Peter and John had started out running at about the same pace, John took the lead and arrived at the tomb first. Just as the women had said, the sealing stone had been rolled back. The grave was wide open. Because John was slow and reflective about everything, he stopped at the door of the tomb and peered in thoughtfully. Peter was not the kind of man who stood outside of any set of circumstances for very long. So he ran right into the place where Jesus had been laid.

Finally, John entered the tomb. Both men stood astonished, gazing straight ahead.

Something inside John's mind seemed to click. *What was it?* he thought. *The sign of the prophet Jonas.* "Yes, that's it. Jesus told us He wouldn't stay dead for long, just as Jonah did not stay in the fish for long."

In a moment, John had the whole thing figured out. He stood there in the quiet reverie of his discovery until his heart was sure. John believed!

"Mary was right. Jesus is gone!" said Peter, unaware of what John had said. "Jesus' body is gone; it's been stolen!"

John stood there shaking his head with a wry smile.

"What's that grinning, idiotic face of yours mean?" asked Peter. He seemed incensed that anyone could laugh at a time like this.

Then John broke into laughter.

Peter was bewildered.

John turned his back on the tomb and began to walk away. Then he stopped. He turned once more and faced the tomb. He threw his young knowing face at the sky and shouted, "Yes!"

"Yes, what?" asked Peter. "Yes what? What are you so happy about?"

"Yes! Yes!" laughed John again. "Jesus is risen. He's alive! . . . Yes!"

Peter's mind had been so dulled by the last several days' events that it took him all of five minutes to understand the truth. When he did, he too began to cry, "Yes! Yes!"

Now there were two of them laughing. The universe was locked in laughter with them. The very tomb itself echoed the grand, "Yes!"

Oh how I would have liked to have seen their rejoicing, but I was not there, . . . sadly, I was not there! ❧

Chapter Four

Peter and John ran fast. Spurred on by their new joy, they far out-distanced Mary. They had come and gone before Mary Magdalene was able to return to the tomb.

Mary finally arrived back at the garden, which lay before the tomb. She was still carrying the spices. Who knows why. Perhaps she thought the missing body would be back. Most likely, she wasn't able to think at all. She just moved in a bewildered frame of mind that allowed her feet to work better than her mind.

She might have carried those spices forever, except for an odd occurrence. As she began to approach the tomb she began to cry. Her tears were a welcomed release for her grief. Jesus was her best Friend. Now, not only was He dead, but someone had desecrated His grave and stolen His body. And for what? There were no riches hidden in His burial garment. Jesus wore no jewelry that might have enticed a grave robber.

She continued her tears right to the door of the shallow cave. Stooping over, she peered into the tomb. Through her teary, blurred vision, she saw two beings dressed in white.

"Woman, why are you crying?" the men asked.

Mary sobbed out a reply, "Someone has stolen the body of my Lord, and I don't know where they have taken it."

Then Mary turned around and saw Jesus. In her grief, she didn't recognize Him. Actually the incredible idea that the dead Jesus was now alive was still too grand a joy to be admitted within the walls of her narrow grieving soul.

He asked her two questions, "Woman, why are you crying? Who are you looking for?"

Mary thought He was the gardener. Then Jesus spoke her name in that personal and unforgettable way that only Jesus could speak, "Mary!"

The quiet word *Mary* awoke an old familiarity. Who was this? The gardener? No. Could it be the Master? No. . . . Perhaps. . . . She dared not accept what she could clearly see. It *is* the Master. He is alive. . . incredible, preposterous, crazy . . . yet, it had to be so! Suddenly the unbelievable truth was believable—Jesus is alive! Mary's dark doubts fell away. Light shot through stone!

"My Teacher!" she cried now smothering her sobs in laughter. Crying and laughter had been typical all through that morning.

Mary was the first person to actually see Jesus alive. She would soon hurry back to blurt out her unbelievable announcement to all. I did not learn till a day later of these early reports. When I did, I was incensed.

It was when Mary began telling others that she had seen the Lord alive that I began having difficulty with the whole story of Jesus' resurrection. That His body had been stolen was unpleasant, but at least it was believable. The idea that Jesus was alive seemed for me preposterous! I chose to be reasonable. I would not be guilty of their madness, and hence I fell into an abyss of my own making. ❧

Chapter Five

According to Mary Magdalene, Jesus left the garden just before one of her friends arrived at the tomb. As strange as it may seem, her friend was also named Mary. Before Mary Magdalene could tell her friend that she had seen the Lord alive, the two angels that had been inside the tomb stepped outside. These two glorious, angelic creatures seemed iridescent in the dim light of morning.

When they stepped out of the tomb, the women fell down with their faces to the ground. Mary Magdalene still clutched the bag of spices to her bosom. Having just seen the resurrected Jesus, she was afraid even to look on the terrifying splendor of the two creatures.

The men spoke, "Why are you here looking for a living man in a dead man's grave? He is not here! He is risen!"

Risen! Even though she had seen the living Christ, the word brought a glorious confidence to Mary and her friend. This confidence erupted into a joy they could hardly contain.

The glistening creatures continued speaking, "Remember what He told you while He was with you in Galilee? He said that He would be killed but would come back to life three days later."

There was a long silence. The eerie quiet caused both Marys to study the ground for a long time.

When they lifted their eyes, the angels had vanished.

"He's alive!" they cried with one voice.

It was only then that Mary Magdalene dropped the spices and said, "We won't be needing these!"

Soon they were telling the news everywhere. As I said, I did not hear the fantastic story for another day or two. But they came that very Sunday to report their joyous discovery to my friends, the apostles. But when I heard their report later, I still did not believe. What I did believe is that both Marys were poor sorrowing women trying to deal with grief in the best way they knew how. Still, they were consistent. They told the same wild tale, the same wild way.

I wish I could have seen those women that Sunday morning. I wish I could have seen their great joy. But I was not there, . . . sadly, I was not there.

Chapter Six

By midafternoon of that never-to-be-forgotten Sunday, the entire world seemed to be in an uproar—a unanimous uproar. The resurrection madness was spreading—the delirium was on the move.

Two of Jesus' friends, however, were traveling to the village of Emmaus where they lived. The tiny town was less than a two-hour walk from Jerusalem. Like more and more of Jesus' friends, they too had heard the buzz that He was alive. While they desperately wanted it to be true, they themselves had not seen Jesus. They were caught in the stretch between a lovely rumor and their own need to see Jesus for themselves. Only then would they fully agree to the story.

As these two friends were walking along talking about Jesus' life and recent execution, they were joined by a stranger. This unnamed companion fell into conversation with them. Jesus sensed their heaviness and felt their hard-to-accept new joy. "What are you two talking about?" asked Jesus as He fell into stride walking with them.

They told Jesus, whom they did not recognize, that they were talking about Jesus of Nazareth. "This Jesus," they said, "though recently killed, has been reported to be alive again."

Jesus began to remind them of all that the ancient prophets had foretold concerning how the Messiah would appear when He came to earth. He was, of course, painting a picture of His own life and resurrection.

Suddenly the warm wayside lecture ended, for the two with whom Jesus traveled, were at their home. Jesus pretended to be going on down the road. But it was time for supper so they begged Him to stay a moment and to share the evening meal with them. Incredible as it may seem, they still had not recognized Him.

Jesus accepted their invitation. Soon after they entered the house, the three of them sat down to eat. It was a simple meal. Jesus reached for a loaf of bread that was on the table, and they watched Him carefully take it in His hands. He broke the loaf of bread in two and then looked up toward the low ceiling of the room and blessed it. But they did not look up. They were stupefied, unable to take their eyes from His hands. For His hands were torn by ugly wounds.

"Mercy! What happened to your hands?!" exclaimed the owner of the house. The loaf fell back to the table. It clattered on the clay plate. Jesus was gone. Joy filled the room, and they began to laugh.

"Yes. . . . Yes!" they laughed.

Oh how I wished I had been there, . . . but sadly, I was not there. ⌘

Chapter Seven

Except for Mary Magdalene, the two men on the road to Emmaus were the first to actually see Jesus alive. But shortly after that, He appeared to all of the apostles—all except me. What occurred at that meeting, the others faithfully reported to me the next day. That's when I also heard the tale of the two travelers who had seen Jesus on Sunday afternoon.

In a single day, my world was upside down. People in whom I had always placed a great deal of confidence were now talking the same kind of nonsense as Mary Magdalene. I can tell you, I'm a man who is not easily taken in by wild tales. Nor do I listen to exaggerations. Never do I stamp fiction as fact. So when the disciples all came to me and said, "We have seen the Lord alive," I can tell you I was more than skeptical, I was irate.

"Listen up! All of you!" I shouted. "Crucified men do not come back to life. It never has been! It never will be! Jesus was a good teacher and a great friend, but He's gone! The kingdom of God was a lovely dream, but it's over. He hung out there last Friday dying by inches till His great heart of love would beat no more. You don't come back from that kind of death. Crucifixions are not temporary inconveniences. They kill! Jesus is dead." I spoke out of desperation. "I'll have no more of your resurrection nonsense till I can personally stick my finger in the wounds in His hands and thrust my hand into His wounded side. Leave me alone until you're back in touch with reality." My words burst forth more to convince myself than others in the room.

They left me. I was glad, but only for a moment.

"God, where are You?" I began to weep. "I'm an honest man, too honest to believe these impossible tales about Jesus. But, oh God, how I wish they were true. I never had a friend like the Master. I would give my soul to see Him one more time. I cannot speak the word *love* except I see His face."

Now I was weeping, alone and uncontrolled.

"If only I had not left Him in Gethsemane. If only I had died on Calvary with Him. If only He was alive, as all of them say He is. If only I had been there when they say He appeared."

But I was not there, . . . sadly, I was not there. 〰

Chapter Eight

Life crept by. Time stopped. For seven days—rather seven long years—I lived in stubborn doubt. Not only did I doubt—I did so loudly. I have always been a man who takes a stand for rational, explainable truth. I became a vile thorn in the mind of all of those who said they had seen Him alive.

The next Sunday I was with the disciples in a sealed room. We had locked ourselves in this room for a measure of security. The officials who crucified Jesus were anxious to seize the rest of us.

Suddenly, the Lord appeared! He was right there in a room where every door was locked. None of the bolted doors had opened, but He was there. His glorious visit sent a shudder of splendor through my body. The hair raised on the nape of my neck.

Then, Jesus turned . . . deliberately toward me.

No, I thought, my knees knocking in fear, *He's actually looking at me.*

Not only did He look at me, but He walked across the room and stood directly in front of me. His eyes met my eyes, and then I lowered mine. The silence of His scrutiny was a weight I never want to bear again, ever.

"Thomas," He said, "reach out your fingers . . . put them into My wounded hands. Take your hand and thrust it into My side, and be no longer a skeptic but believe."

Hot tears warmed by the fire of my ugly denials burned their way across my face. I dropped to my knees and sobbed. Suddenly the light from His eyes pierced my soul and I understood.

From the depths of my heart I cried, "My Lord and my God!"

The days of my exile were over. I had seen Him alive. I was there. I believed. Finally, I was as filled with joy as all the rest.

The days of my new joy gradually passed from high elation about the living Jesus to feelings of impassioned obligation. Jesus didn't want us merely to celebrate His coming back to life as though it were something to make us feel good. He wanted the whole world to feel alive. He wanted everyone to celebrate the same glorious truth we were celebrating. He wanted people in other lands and coming ages to see that it was not just *His* death He had conquered. *All death* had been forever conquered. Nobody would ever again have to die and remain death's victim.

After a few weeks Jesus left us to return to heaven. But there could be no mistaking what He expected of those He left on earth. He commanded us to tell the whole world—every man, woman, and child—about this wonderful, new, everlasting life.

I, Thomas, bear you this witness, for loving Jesus is knowing that resurrection life can never be killed. Such life will splinter crosses and split tombs! Hate may wound life, but nothing can ever destroy it. Just as each new springtime wakes the frozen earth with flowers, so every sunrise shouts the wonder: Death is temporary. Life in Him is forever! YES! ⚘

"Because you have seen me,
you have believed;
blessed are those who have not seen
and yet believed."

JOHN 20:29